Our Flag Was Still There

Other books by Richard Tillinghast

Sleep Watch (1969)
The Knife and Other Poems (1980)

WESLEYAN POETRY

Our Flag Was Still There

Poems by
Richard Tillinghast

Wesleyan University Press
Middletown, Connecticut

These poems have previously appeared in the following periodicals:

"Our Flag Was Still There," *New England Review & Bread Loaf Quarterly.*

"Fossils, Metal, and the Blue Limit," lines 1–99, *The Harvard Advocate.* The entire poem, *Tendril.*

"Earthquake Story," *Sumac.*

"Sewanee in Ruins," *Ploughshares.*

"Easter Week: Vermont," *Antaeus,* and in England, *Critical Quarterly.*

"Envoi," *Harvard Magazine.*

Lines 1–31 of "Fossils, Metal, and the Blue Limit" were printed as a pamphlet by White Creek Press, North Bennington, Vermont, 1982.

"Sewanee in Ruins" was printed as a chapbook by The University Press, Sewanee, Tennessee. First edition, 1981; second edition, 1983.

"Easter Week: Vermont" was printed as a broadside by Palaemon Press, Winston-Salem, North Carolina, 1982.

All inquiries and permissions requests should be addressed to the Publisher, Wesleyan University Press, 110 Mt. Vernon Street, Middletown, Connecticut 06457

Distributed by Harper & Row Publishers, Keystone Industrial Park, Scranton, Pennsylvania 18512

LIBRARY OF CONGRESS CATALOGING IN PUBLICATION DATA

Tillinghast, Richard.
    Our flag was still there.
    I. Title.
PS3570.I3809 1984 811'.54 83-25965
ISBN 0-8195-5106-6 (alk. paper)
ISBN 0-8195-6099-5 (pbk. : alk. paper)

Manufactured in the United States of America

First Edition

First Wesleyan Paperback Edition

This book is for
Mary, Joshua, Julia, Andrew,
and Charles Tillinghast

Contents

Our Flag Was Still There

Our Flag Was Still There

For music, "Victory at Sea," or "In the Mood."

"Chessie," the Chesapeake and Ohio's
advertising mascot, snoozes
under sixty-mile-per-hour lamplight.
Two tabby kittens gaze saucer-eyed at their tomcat dad,
who sits alertly on his haunches,
soft fieldcap cocked to one side above neat,
pleasure-pursed lips and regimental whiskers.
One paw bandaged.
A Congressional Medal of Honor
red-white-and-blue-ribboned around his neck.
As convincingly at attention as a military-style,
family-oriented cat can be in a pullman car.
On his well-groomed chest, rows of campaign ribbons.
A dignified, "can do" look
hovers about his muscled smile.

In the luggage rack, a U.S. combat helmet
and a rising-sun flag in tatters.

I had a flag like that.
One of my three red-headed Marine cousins
brought it back from the South Pacific.
I thumbtacked it to the wall of my room.
The Japanese who had fought under it
perished in fierce firestorms.
They and their flag went up in that conflagration.

Our flag was still there.
Against a backdrop of blue sky and innocent clouds,
a line of six blunt-nosed P-47 fighters —
boxy and powerful like the grey Olds
we bought after the War
and drove to the Berkshires for the summer —
flew off on a mission to Corregidor.
The flag, unfurled in the stiff breeze,
was superimposed over the line of airplanes
on the cover of the Sunday magazine
one June morning in 1943.
The wind that made it wave as it does in pictures
blew off long ago toward Japan.

The sun nooned over orange groves and beaches.
Sparks from welding torches
illuminated the sleep of the City of the Angels
and darkened the sleep of others
as women workers beside the men
lowered masks over their faces,
and the children of New Jersey and Mississippi,
Europe and Detroit,
labored to make aluminum fly
and set afloat fleets of destroyers
and submarines radaring to the kill.

Looking ahead, there was a world of blue-grass lawns,
paneled wood enameled white, grandparents' faces
rosy over reassuring, hand-rubbed bannisters,
Yale locks, brass door-knockers, hardwood floors,
the odor of good furniture and wax,
a holiday design of holly leaves and berries on a stiff card,
a little girl holding gift packages as big as she is,
a boy, a real boy, bright as a new penny.

But now, in '43, the men and women pulled apart
like the elders of some stern, taboo-ridden tribe,
putting off till after the War the lives
of those who in twenty-five years
stood baffled on the 4th of July among uncles,
drove good German cars,
floated in tubs of hot, redwood-scented water with friends,
and greeted each other with the word, "Peace."

Fossils, Metal, and the Blue Limit

"Thou anointest my head with oil."

The sky, out of reach, unexpected,
like the curved ceiling of a mosque—
us motoring up the long freeway
north from San Francisco:
a promise, yes, a blue ribbon.

We navigate privileged space in the fast lane,
two men and two boys in a Volkswagen van,
alongside families getting a jump on the weekend heat
in cushy, portable, air-conditioned interiors
that rolled down suburban drives
hours and miles ago.
My big, hot-rodded, 1700-cubic-centimeter engine revs
fast, loud, and *comme il faut;*
the van lunges eagerly northstate

breezing through a river of air—
inches above the concrete slabs that,
dovetailed by sky-colored slicks of asphalt, *are*
the freeway.

Three fiberglass poles and a nine-foot, willowy fly rod
of the lightest material made
bounce easily to the even pace of the engine
as my customized classic
1966 VW Microbus, forest green
with white trim,
or as I might call it
in moments of gloom,
"decrepit old wreck," —
burns through the blue fumes
with bumperstickers advising contradictorily "Bomb Iran"
and "Think Trout."
Tolstoy would have loved it.

Everything the round eye sees
suggests the absence of limitation
as we uncork the day with coffee and Bushmill's —
even what the shapeless, mind's eye
imagines and recalls:
the view to limestone in the pine-shadowed creek
under Mount Lassen,
our destination;
even the fat, springy, uncoiling, muscular
earthworms I dug at first light out of odorous humus
with a clean-tined pitchfork.

Ayub, *né* Borsky,
companion on many an outing,
fair or foul, poaching or sport, trout or shark—:
street artist, carpenter, taxi driver, mystic, bad cook,
with a face like a rained-on rock, —
rolls a cigarette out of thick, dark
Dutch tobacco,
smokes it through his Mosaic beard
(his grey hair thin, stretched and stranded,
three wavy pencil-lines over his crown),
and gives his well-considered philosophy of life
and trout
to his two sons,
Eric—dark, humorous, fourteen,
maker of fine model airplanes—
and Dylan—blond, ten—:

about "feeding stations," about how
the big trout take the choicest spots
("Just like you, Dad"),
how they face upstream, treading icy water,
and don't blink—
about the trout's "window of vision"
wherein the fisherman looms huge, dark, and threatening
("Just like you again, Dad")
unless he treads softly, and relies on concealment—
and how "the freeway is a river,"
the cars swimming in four diverted and weaving currents,
how everything is like that really,
and how—

Quick as a rainbow trout
flashes sunlight
out of a deep pool—
right at the top of a grade
past Cloverdale,
the green warning signal on the dash flickers
and stays lit!
Blue smoke congregates behind us,
I veer across two lanes,
slide to a stop on the sandy shoulder,
hood
(in the back in a Volkswagen, remember?)
up,
head under hood,
smoke in eyes:
OIL! the engine-opening black
as the underground streams
of Arabia, black
as the fingernails and secret dreams
of the Ayatollah.

We glut it with an extra quart, then another,
and point it toward the exit
though it smokes
like a pointillist painting of London weather
and early Marxist pollution-stacks.

Like those long first paragraphs of *Bleak House,*
creeping, deliberate, ominous,
we nose the cloud
into the town of Weed
along a cyclone fence and frontage road,
up a little paved crescent of street,
then down another one, plain and straight,
in view of the bleached, horizontal, meandering river—
then straight down, miraculously, a yarrow-wild drive:
two wheel-thin slabs of concrete wheelwise
downhill, beside an abandoned, pink, shotgun house.

Down a slanting, weed-jungled drive,
beside a pink house that is having no trouble
falling apart,
under two shapely, identical camphor trees
and one disreputable sycamore,
next to a grey picket fence and a rained-on, broke-down couch,
we squat on our heels like aborigines
sun-squinting at the engine: black, oil-flooded.
Groping behind it blind I scorch
the first, second, third knuckles on overheated steel,
grabbing for the burst, expensive cooler hose
splashing black fossil-oil
over every inch of metal,
where it burns off as blue smoke
into the clogged atmosphere.

My Piscean friend grins
in the dirty face of disaster.
(Of course it is not *his* car.)

Hi-temp rubber hose, this size (handing it),
and three quarts 30-weight oil—
the boys are out of the van then,
skateboarding down the long street.
"The sky's the limit"
is the thought I imagine
for them.
For us, a problem, a headache, gloom.

We take in the panorama
of blue-collar suburbia:
cheap, 1950s houses
dwarfed more even than they anyway would be
by "recreational vehicles," evil-looking, smoked-glass vans,
reptilian-fendered hot rods, a vintage Airstream
trailer, jacked-up
Camaros and Mustangs, souped-up
otherworldly Harleys with chrome out to here,
a single, monstrous, ark-sized, blunt-nosed speedboat,
ready to lumber off into the next flood.

Then a (unique in my experience) residential used-car lot,
and a thirtyish, drunkish ex-biker
with a jack to rent—
slouched in the doorway
with "Born to Lose" and "WHITE
ON" and prison-art swastikas
tattooed asymmetrically across his belly,
latitude unknown, longitude uncertain,
where "Save the Whales"
would have seemed more appropriate.
"Hitler's Revenge," he calls my car.
I see the look of concern
drift across my face,
mirrored in the blue sky
of his mirror shades.

But everything's cool!

The procedure:
battery disconnected, jittery, wires pulled
off and labeled with bits of brown tape.
Yank off the gas-line, gas spurts,
choke it fumblingly with an old pencil (not knowing
to clamp it first
with your small vise-grip),
and it dangles there sealed—

pass the Bushmill's around
(cuts the fumes):
then to get the bumper and assorted pieces of tin,
cunningly shaped,
from around the engine, *then,*
passing the big wrench back and forth between us,
and dropping it once, twice, clangingly on cement:
four nuts haltingly and bothersomely
twisted off the engine-studs,
while the neighbors—two Bahai housewives,
the over-the-hill Angel, and an off-duty postman—
drink beer and make free with advice,
we ease, rock, nudge
the engine onto the ton-and-a-half
Hein-Becker floor-jack,
hulking and out of place,
mired and sliding already
in the sweet grass
becoming mud.

The disconnected engine broods there like a primal force,
the metal like a fifth element,
like an alien life-form from a slower planet
putting in downtime—
earth-morning becoming midday
as the metal ticks and bangs, cooling, contracting,
under twin camphor trees and sky.

Were days like this foreseen
in the Platonic heaven of machinists?—
or by the generations of men,
with boots and soiled caps and wire-rimmed eyeglasses
and daughters and sons,
who brought iron ore out of the earth,
learned to smelt it, and formed it into steel,
then refined oil to cool
every frictive articulation of that wonder,
an apparatus (1637) for applying mechanical power,
consisting of a number of parts, each
having a definite function,—
which they had named *Machine?*

The day heats up,
mare's-tails braid across the blue.
The boys skate back into sight down the long, straight street
exhilarated, with motor oil and lengths of hose.
Now, pull the old hoses off,
fit the new ones on true,
tighten the clamps to a turn,—
pump the jack,
grunt, puff, and stagger,
bring the boys and neighbors into it,
struggle, despair, and struggle
to work the heavy, lumbering mass of old technology
onto the four, eccentrically placed engine-studs,
tighten the four nuts back on,
cross-eyed with concentration,
feeling humbly resigned
and at the same time in some sense weirdly lucky,
that nothing worse than this
has gone wrong,—
                    fit

the tin back on,
hook up the gas-line,
plug the wires back in,
replace the bumper, and our job is done.

Now the blond, virgin oil
inside the newly tight engine.
Now I reach out my hand
and turn the key.
The engine kicks to life,
no oil leaks,
the stream awaits.
In a moment, you who read this,
you can drive it to the carwash and clean it up for me.

My hand, arm, shoulder muscles rebound
with freedom, reflexively,
from the work they have done:
and the quaint construance of the word *nut*
which follows its botanical meanings
in the Oxford English Dictionary
(I wish I had it right here at my elbow)—
a small block of wood, iron, etc.,
pierced, and wormed with a female screw—
drifts into my mind,
suggesting the history, and the slow romance
of machinery.

Maybe what I mean to say is the way oil
looks on skin:
black, verging on chemically murky translucence,
the little human hairs bravely standing up half-bent
beneath the grime, the irreducible petro-dirt—
or maybe it's what is going to happen
to Joe Borsky,
how two weeks from now
he will take a knife in the gut
and be in all the papers
as he and the passenger in his cab
go after a man who is trying to further
the evolution of the human race,
for God's sake,
by raping a nurse
as she goes home from work
on Nob Hill at four in the morning.

He's one of the lucky ones, however:
only his flesh is wounded.
He'll soon recover.

Waiting for you,
so we can get on up the road,
I loaf here in the bruised, oil-shiny grass,
with a green pen that writes blue,
while my friend meditatively smokes,
as unaware as I am of what lies ahead of him.
The boys are quiet now, the neighbors
have gone home
with their jack, their help, and their noise.
Smells of crushed grass, beer, hot oil, scorched metal
hang in the air.

I hear the river
loop and crook back on itself
over its sandy-bottomed channel
through the nearby field,
where shattered cinderblocks
and an old transmission sprawl.

Between the river and the sky,
the mountains:
the Sierra—a myth, a truth,
the hard backbone of the West,
distances extending untraveled
a thousand miles or more from here
up switchbacked roads
with pine needles dusted over them,
over daylong, empty deserts,
past granite diners that say more
than will easily go into words—
to the eastern slope of the Rockies,
half of America away.

Stained with the bodies of half-billion-year-old plants,
releasing my breath upward,
I stare upward uncomprehendingly
at the blue, cloud-woven limit of the sky.

Earthquake Story

The cabin at sunset.

Nothing had changed or faded! How simple it now seemed. All the solutions, all the things you took up for a while, then dropped—the anxiety that at times seemed to wire up into hysteria, the hours spent going over the charts, those days were over forever.

Once they had decided to get there, getting here was no problem. Time on the road condenses into its own kind of eternity. Paranoia vis-à-vis the Texas Highway Rangers, the bloodcurdling hatred of the Turks, being awake with the alarm clock at five, slowly making the grade over deathly beautiful Virginia hills in the fog, that Ohio River hotel while repairs were being made, all this evaporated into a cloud of consciousness not the size of a monkey's fist in the great sea of time—just as they say a drowning man relives his entire life in a flash, all this vanished before the first trivial chores and considerations.

They had made themselves pretty comfortable during the course of the day. We'll skip that part. At three they were tired of being cooped up inside and went down for a paper: *The Gommorah Gazette*. Somehow the car wouldn't start and they had to leave the car there, etc., etc. What had been revealed to them as truth was revealed to be lies. (Realistic passage in which three electric heaters in succession break down much to consternation, fire begins to go out. The wood is wet, or frozen. Argument over whether wood can freeze.)

She began to glow like an hibiscus snake, he ran through several fortunes in a score of years. They forgot about the weekend, the earthquake itself became a memory. His coats were never, what began as a scare gave way to a chicken, these bodies themselves will be indistinguishable from air, the suction along a mushroom's skin.

There we were.
All alone.

Sewanee in Ruins

for Andrew Lytle

Ongietan sceal gléaw hæle   hú gæstlíc bið,
þonne eall þisse worulde wela   wéste stondeð,
swá nú missenlíce   geond þisne middangeard
winde biwáune   weallas stondaþ,
hríme bihrorene,   hryðge þá ederas.
Wóriað þá wínsalo,   waldend licgað
dréame bidrorene.

> (A wise man should understand how full of ghosts it
>   will be
> when all the good things of this world are in ruins—:
> just as now, throughout this middle-earth,
> walls stand windswept,
> wrapped about with rime,—the storm-beaten buildings
>   of men.
> The banqueting-halls collapse; the lords lie
> deprived of joy.
> —*The Wanderer*, 11.72–79a)

Ecce quam bonum et quam iucundum
habitare fratres in unum.
—Psalm 133

... bare ruin'd quires...
—Shakespeare

I.

The Romantics were right.
Gothic buildings are best seen in ruin:
sky-sprung clerestories in wild brambles,
Romanesque arches reconstructed by the mind,
tumbled-over stones to stumble on in a field
of grey violets,
in a place you can no longer drive to.

When I walk by the Neo-Gothic
duPont Library at the University of the South,
its new stone rouged-up, peachy
after October rain,
my mind sees the façade stripped of half its masonry
by Virginia creeper and torn fog.
I smile into leaves of the bramble stock,
strong and ugly,
aggressively shiny in the mist.

But I come from the cemetery,
where the past is buried under stone.
I smile into the broad, pleasant faces of my students,
the black among the white
—for we are one people—;
yet my thoughts are with men I have heard of and read of
who, possessed by a fatal romanticism,
killed at fourteen,
ate corn burned in the field,
and wore the dead enemies' shoes
in 1865, when everything burned
but the brick chimneys
and a way of talking.

I touch with my tongue my four gold teeth,
answer to the name *Sir,*
and feel out of place
in my twenty-year-old tweeds
among these boys and girls
who call themselves men and women,
these ripe-peach bodies and untouched smiles,
these peacock-blue, canary-yellow, billiard-table-green
clothes from the catalogue of L. L. Bean—
initials emblazoned as on silver—
and hundreds of tiny alligators that never snap.

I climb the 1890s Gothic battlements to my classroom
and teach these fortunate young men and women
their history,
and the old lost nation's name for this spot:
Rattlesnake Springs.
Two coiled rattlesnakes spelled into a slab of rock.

Saawaneew in Algonquin,
though white men didn't know it,
meant The South,
from the Ohio to the Gulf of Mexico.

The words of someone's old diary or letter from 1860:
Nine bishops in their robes
and 50 or 60 clergymen in surplices and gowns
and some 5,000 people
formed a procession
and headed by a band playing Hail Columbia
marched to the spot
where the main building of the university
was to be.
Here Old Hundred was sung by the vast multitude.

Those confident, cotton-flush Southerners,
fifty years from the wilderness,
with their horse races, cockfights, African slaves,
their *code of duello and decanter,*
their railroad cars full of Sir Walter Scott romances,
their 19th-century optimism
and half a million cotton dollars as endowment,
founded *their "Southern Oxford,"*
as they always called it.

The hogsheads of hams, the barrels, and boxes, and bags
of groceries, the cartloads of crockery and glass, the
bales of sheeting and blankets, and acres of straw beds,
indicated that Southern hospitality for once
had entered upon the difficult undertaking
of outdoing itself....

Yet even then,
there was a feeling as of a great danger
near at hand,
a yawning chasm which all feared to look upon....

Next April
the bells of St. Philip's and St. Michael's,
the old Charleston churches,
chain-rang in celebration.
But a clearheaded observer, if one could be found,
looking off the Battery past Fort Sumter
into the immense ocean and sky,
must have felt mostly dread.

The rest of the oft-told tale is too well known,
how war devastated the land
the two armies passed over, fighting as they went.
The frame houses
built for Bishops Elliott and Polk
have been burnt to the ground,
the cornerstone blasted to pieces by Federal troops—
the six-ton block of marble
that 34 yoke of oxen
had dragged up the mountain from Elk River.

We are encamped (21st Indiana Infantry)
on the top of the Cumberland Mountains,
on the site of the grand Southern University
that was to have been. . . .
Near our quarters is a very large spring
of the clearest and finest water I ever drank.
We expect no real fight between here and Atlanta.

My pleasant-faced freshmen
from South Carolina, Texas, Kentucky, Alabama
laugh at the word *Yankee,*
considering my use of it a kind of local color.
To them the Great War of the Sixties
is like some football game we lost.

And I have no quarrel with them.

To wear expensive clothes,
to enjoy wearing them
—or just not to think about it—,
to go through the seasons as from one party to the next,
to know no enemies,
to turn from boy or girl May- or June-like
into man or woman,
to make 18-year-old love in the back seat of a Cadillac
on a warm Delta night—
this is the way to be young!

Not to ride and kill with Forrest all across Tennessee
or die with Jackson at Chancellorsville
or Polk at Pine Mount,
or come back from war
with health and nerves and worldly goods destroyed.

The privilege of being young,
the luxury of ignoring history—
this is what their great-great-grandfathers fought for,
though they lost.

For the flaw in their Neoclassical structure—
the evil of owning human beings—,
they paid, all of them and all of us,
punished by a vengeance only New England could devise—
though only three Tennesseans out of a hundred in 1860
had owned a slave.

The Armies of Emancipation,
having *loosed the fateful lightning
of His terrible swift sword,*
would be free to go West and kill Indians.
The machines tooled in that war economy
eased the North on plush velvet and iron rails
into its Gilded Age,
and reconstructed the South
with sharecropping and hunger—
and a deeper thirst,
not satisfied by the Coke you drink
flying Delta over kudzu fields out of Atlanta,
reading *The Last Gentleman* by Walker Percy.

History stopped in 1865,
then started again as memory:
the grey and gold of the good-smelling, broadcloth uniform,
the new, beautiful, handsewn battle-flag,
the West Point strategists, the Ciceronian orations,
the cavalry charges—
soldiers on a road sing "Away, Away"—;
then the heads shot off friends' shoulders,
the desertions, the belly-killing stench of dead flesh,
the forced marches over hardscrabble Virginia roads—
and Richmond like a brick graveyard.

II.

Gladly they turned
from the tragedy of six years gone
to peaceful forests.
Yet for many, old at twenty, life seemed a phantasmagoria;
and Cupid stumped on crutches.
They took mint from the cold, cave-mouth springs
and drank in the cool evenings,
and drank in the warm afternoons,
or dozed and dreamed, the ruined ladies, the widows
among lavender and orrisroot and plain pine boards,
and the one grain of opium from a small silver box.
And some of them died early, and the families died,
leaving us only initials on a well-made old steamer trunk
or a curious name cut into stone above a grave,
and two 19th-century hands clasping in marble.

But some had the faith,
or had the pluck,
to come back from disaster and build.
Charles Todd Quintard, 2nd Bishop of Tennessee:
We recited the Apostles' Creed
and made the oaks and hickories ring
with the Gloria in Excelsis.
As our procession entered the modest, wood-frame chapel,
the nine students in their drab, twice-turned suits,
the four professors in their purple and scarlet
Oxford hoods or neat, faded Confederate uniforms,
I stepped aside
to allow the plasterer to go out
with his mortar board and trowel.

Robert Dabney of Powhatan County, Virginia,
Professor of Metaphysics and English Literature.
William Mercer Green, 1st Bishop of Mississippi.
General, later Chaplain, Shoup—from Ohio.
Major George Rainsford Fairbanks,
a dogged, determined, relentless, humble
follower of idealists—
which is not quite the same as,
though it may be rarer than, an idealist.
Josiah Gorgas, head of ordnance under Lee.
Edmund Kirby Smith,
the last Confederate general to surrender,
Professor of Pure Mathematics and Botany.

Later came Dr. DuBose,
a tiny silver saint who lived elsewhere,
more conversant with the tongues of angels
than of men.
Sitting on the edge of his desk in his black gown,
talking haltingly of Aristotle, he would suspend,
rapt, in some mid-air beyond our ken,
murmuring, "The starry heavens. . . ."
We, with a glimpse of things,
would tiptoe out of the classroom.

Mr. Wadhams, of the Coldstream Guards,
six feet two, blue-eyed, brick-cheeked:
the village baker.
Monsieur Pillet, the tailor,
who built a fine house here:
Your suit makes me think of two French cities,
Toulouse and Toulon.

The century turned, and brought Dr. Henneman:
passionate, black-bearded, bespectacled,
with an adoration for Beowulf, *Chaucer, Shakespeare,*
a grimace for Dr. Donne,
and more important, a capacity for furious
moral tantrums—
his beard on end clear out to his ears,
he would beat the desk with his fist and roar:
"My God, gentlemen, do something!*"*

And then there were "the ladies":
Miss Fanny Preston, the only woman
who made Moultrie Guerry's *Men Who Made Sewanee.*
Miss Lily Green, the Bishop's daughter.
Miss Sallie Milhado,
with her picayune cigarettes and mint juleps,
her squirrel-tail hat and her thunder storms.
And Miss Sada Elliott, about whom it was said
that *a hopeless love affair with her*
was one of the required courses at the University.
They were the yeast that made the cake rise,
and knew it,
and said so,
but in private.

They brought their pride, and planted gardens—
those low-country, low-church aristocrats.
More than one man
whose London-made, silver-damascened shotgun
had never shot anything meaner than pheasant,
roamed the deep woods alone
hunting squirrel and rabbit to feed his family.

Around their dinner tables in the barnlike frame halls
that they built from the cheap local timber,
they reconstructed a life
out of kindness and old silver and good conversation,
teaching manners, piety, and learning
in that order
to boys whose land-poor families sent them here,
often on credit,
seeing them becoming too countrified and ignorant
now that their world had fallen.

When the back-country folk from Tickbush and Lost Cove,
Jumpoff and Shake-rag Hollow
came around selling eggs, furs, and moonshine,
they spoke Scots and English dialects
that had disappeared into the hills
two hundred years before,
and they quoted their prices in shillings.

Men's eyes in these mountains
look into you
as if they were sighting you
along the barrel of a gun. . . .

In the summer of "70" and "71"
the white laboring men of the town,
led by a desperado named Rose,
undertook to run all the Negroes off the mountain.
A Negro carpenter who worked for Mr. Dabney
was almost cut to pieces
and left for dead
on the site of Otey Memorial Church.

This village was now the *res publica*
—all that was left of it—
to men who had led armies.
They governed with firmness
and something more:
For nights the streets were patrolled by the students
under command of Colonel Sevier.
His hands were kept full
for the depot element was perfectly lawless
and some of the students were almost as bad.
Colonel Sevier put down the trouble at the depot
by walking into Rose's cabin and arresting him,
though his friends were about him
and pistols were plentiful in the air.

Sewanee was still not much more
than an open place in the dense woods,
dusty and muddy by season,
with a field cleared for baseball:

If an angel from heaven came to the mountain
we would say, that he came "up to Sewanee,"
yet when people do come up
they find spectre-like or aldermanic hogs
roaming the University,
bringing up interesting *families in our alleys,*
or lounging, sybaritically, in mud-puddles.

P. S. to an old letter:
I do beg you, my dear Major,
to have ye undergrowth cut
in front of your house.
It will give that quarter such a civilised *look.*

And the students?
They could be discovered *amiably and discreetly*
behind closed doors on the third floor,
playing not flutes or lyres or even saxophones,
but poker.
Still others will be bowed over a table,
vexed to the soul with the return of Xenophon
or the fall, too long delayed, of a certain empire.
A few will be off in the valley
bargaining for a beverage called mountain dew. . . .
Later they will have consumed their purchase
to the last sprightly drop
and will be bawling out deplorable ballads
and pounding tables
and putting crockery to uncouth noisy uses
in the neighborhood of one or another of the old ladies
who will appear scandalized as expected. . . .

But not everyone felt as much at home
as did the boys, the old ladies, and the pigs—
like the music teacher from Massachusetts
back in 1869:
I am among rebels!
They are only overcome and not subdued.
In Spirit, language, conduct, feeling,
in all essential things they are rebels
as truly today as when the Arch-traitor Jeff Davis
was on the throne of their bogus Confederacy.
Their names for all Northerners
are "Northern Infidels", "Mercenary Vandals",
"Scum of the earth", etc., etc.
They are Bombastic, ignorant, lazy & defiant,
and the women
are the very personification
of His Satanic Majesty. . . .

III.

Lineage had nothing to do with their renown,
Mrs. Sanborn wrote;
'Twas ever personality that counted at Sewanee.
(Her subject was Sewanee dogs.)
And if money meant more than we feel it will
in Heaven, —
doesn't it do that when lacking?
Family, dear to "all sorts and conditions,"
took pride of place.

As in any
human utopia,
the soul was free to follow its own bent or warp,
to be eccentric, kind, queer, ornery, plain, or even good.
There were miles of room for wit,
even for artful malice and scandal:
Wonderful the amount of gossip with such scanty material.
The snowball comparison is inadequate.

"The Forks":
A huge, pinky, brown house with pinkier, brownier windows,
flanked by two cottages in which dwell 13 young bipeds.
The family consist of Judge Phelan, his four daughters,
and a little rip of a son.
The Judge is an obstinate, conceited old Irishman.
As for the daughters,
their ages are rather misty.
They range themselves between fifteen and 22—
but some inconvenient old family friends
who were here last summer
put them between 20 and 30.

"Chestnut Hill":
A square white house with green blinds,
an unlovely porch and not the sign of a shade tree
save a few freshly planted saplings.
A straight gravel path leading from a fancy gate,
set in a rail fence,
terminates at the foot of a square pair of steps.
This is called "Chestnut Hill",
because all the saplings are oak.

Snippets of a letter from Miss Sada Elliott
to her brother
at what one might have expected to be
the tender age of 22,
describing "the corporation,"
its houses and its people, in 1871,
with a keen eye for both
(though *jaundiced* might substitute for *keen*).

The Holmes family,
consisting of Mr. and Mrs. Lucien Holmes
and numerous pet canaries:
Mrs. Holmes looks like Aunt Emma, rather "wilferish",
and has old "Lucien dear" quite under hack.
"Old Solution", as the boys call him,
is a fat, sleek, crawly sort of man,
kisses his wife on all occasions,
besides all this is a dunder head.

The widow Polk,
a distant cousin of our friends,
is a commonsense, proper, dignified,
kindhearted widow-woman,
who never meddles in other people's business.
She lives in a melancholy, mulatto-colored,
wooden house with pink blinds, named Waverly.
The front yard is trampled into a desert,
only redeemed by the shade trees, a dilapidated rail fence
and no gate.
She has three little children and keeps house for 26 boys.

The Dabney family:
1st, Mrs. Dabney, a large, handsome, loudvoiced,
kindhearted, tactless, managing, meddling woman.
2ndly, 6 children. 3rd, Miss Marye, Mrs. D's sister.
4th, Professor Dabney, a dear, delightful, abstracted,
over-run, learned, entertaining, over-worked man, —delicate,
refined and venerable looking, although only 38.
Both the Dabneys and Miss Jones are refined. Mrs. Polk
is a little western—all lack polish except Mr. D.
They live in a melancholy, weather-stained, unpainted
barnlike edifice, named Alabama....

The Elliotts (wrote Sada Elliott),
a very queer sort of family, to tell the truth,
have just moved into their new house.
The style is Gothic, color pale lemon, trimming white.
The place is named "Saints Rest".
Mrs. Elliott is a most charming old lady of the old school,
perfectly indescribable,
intensely pleased with and proud of all her children
except the second daughter Miss Sada,
of whom she is a little doubtful.

Her son "the doctor" is a good looking,
stiff young man, very well satisfied with himself
and all his belongings,
but this last seems to be a family trait.
Miss Hesse, the "wheelhorse" of the concern,
runs the machine and bothers the chaplain,
makes him feel queer on the left side....
Miss Charlotte, very highchurch as to theory,
has a little too much grecian bend,
but generally liked....

Mrs. Elliott, secunda,
is a commonplace little woman,
kindhearted and amiable,
but very fussy and wanting in tact,
rather a grooved out mind,
and wanting in decision.

Last comes Miss Sada—
not at all lacking in the family trait
of self-complacency,
very contrary to everyone and everything,
and very obstinate—
rather selfish and supercilious, quite a tease,
not very intimate with anything
but her own shadow. . . .

Next to the Elliotts come the Gorgas family
consisting of the General, commonly called "Old Spot",
Mrs. G. and six children,
dubbed by Miss Sada, the little "Gorgi".

The father is a medium sized man, not very pretty,
walks pigeon-toed and as though on eggs.
His mind runs in a straight line, fixed so at West Point,
and has never been known to deviate.

Mrs. G. is about the same size as the General,
not quite so pretty, rather tragic and "soft soddery",
walks a great deal with her knees—
reminds me a little of Miss Flite, in Bleak House.

Four of the Gorgi
are girls, reminding one strongly of
the little Kenwigses in Nicholas Nickleby.
Their walk is rather a cross between father and mother,

which makes it a spasmodic creep;
they are uglier
than both,
but quite nice children on the whole.

The Chaplain, Gen. Shoup, lives with them—
he is as erratic
as the clouds—thin, good-looking,
smart, pleasant, honest, frank, distracted,

and very intimate at the Elliotts';
wears long coat-tails, has thin legs and they never go
in the same direction,
reminds one of a wind-mill.

The Fairbankses live just where the Polks used to.
As the Major *behaved so* gallantly *in the war*
he has named his place "Rebel's Rest". . . .
They are as they were,

only a little more so.

There was even room for
a Mr. Lee Cotten,
called handsome but looks like a barber's apprentice,
greasy waving hair that falls poetically low on his brow,
"a killing moustache" and bad teeth,
keeps a wholesale grocery down by the depot. . . .

But now as my paper has given out, I will desist.
You look all worn out with my uncharitable rundown.
But it is *all* true.

IV.

Most of the old buildings are gone now—
you can blame fire, or progress, or both:

Forensic Hall, known to some as "Frenzy,"
built by the students in 1874,
demolished before the first World War:
Forensic and dancing—
thermometer two degrees above zero. The cotillion:
Five couples plus two stags,
the hall tastefully decorated
with oil stoves used as partners on the odd dances,
costumes, furs, galoshes.
Finally the piano froze, and,
as the society column would say,
"The last ball of the season,
marking the approach of Lent,
came gracefully to a close."

Powhatan of course: General Kirby Smith's house—
burned in 1956 by *unknown hands*
who, mysteriously and somewhat incongruously,
later moved out of the state.

Magnolia, where we learned languages:
torched by a student who liked to watch things burn.

Van Ness, with its peculiar residents,
its maze of odd apartments
and little porcelain signs in French,
demolished in 1963.

Bairnwick, built later, in 1925,
on the site of Bishop Knight's house, Greyfriars,
is missing its family now
and houses Christians who "encounter"
and pray standing up—
grand in its way, made of flagstone,
like a country house in the Cotswolds,
where Mrs. Myers held court,
with her English bulldog Hrothgar—
who died "contesting the passage of a truck"—
and her recitations of Tennyson's "Ring Out, Wild Bells"
every New Year's Eve.

And the stone and shingle house at Morgan's Steep,
built for Mr. Oertel, the painter,
is shipshape again, with a new roof and new floors—
near the site where John Hunt Morgan,
hotly pursued by Yankee cavalry,
galloped off the sandstone bluff
with important dispatches in his saddlebags
into the tops of black oaks and tulip poplars—:
an old story but not a true one,
we learn, after these years of telling it.

A tiny, anomalous window
almost to the ceiling of the ballroom-sized studio
overlooks it from the study where I write:
put there, some say,
so his adoring daughter
could watch him paint from her playroom.
Or, in the jaundiced view,
so Mrs. Oertel
could keep a custodial eye
on the painter
and the models for his masterpiece,
"The World, the Flesh, and the Devil,"
which stretched over one whole wall of the studio

and later hung in All Saints' Chapel,
where "the Flesh" in question,
a gorgeous, full-length nude,
made compulsory chapel less of a burden
to generations of boys,
as they fasted and prayed "in the beauty of holiness"
or dozed in the back pews
and broke their fast with sweet rolls
behind their *Times*es.

Not far from the Steep,
after one of Ewing Carruthers' notorious soirées,
Harrison Holmes,
perhaps imitating General Morgan's perhaps fictional leap
(Harrison's middle name isn't Lightcap for nothing)
almost flew his Impala convertible
off the side of the mountain.

So many old names, half-forgotten, half-remembered—
like Miss Mary Miller,
with her strange and lovely Chinese face,
romantic birth, and most Victorian outlook,
whose name is carved on the stone arch
over the cemetery gate.

What flesh and blood,
what whispers, what glances, what twists of fate,
are wrapped in words!

Remember "Chestnut Hill"?
It's that old ruin out behind
where the Academy used to be—
a white house in the Classic Revival style,
with a green roof and severe lines overgrown.

Bishop Boone of China named the place Wyndcliff Hall
and planted an avenue of trees along its front line,
"to protect the house from the dust and noise
of passing horse-and-wagon traffic."
Bishop Schereshevski,
while recovering from a long illness,
translated the Bible into Chinese there.

Rooms, porches and passageways grew
about the original building.
Stairways were fetched indoors and led suddenly upward
to platforms of unexplained use,
and to dark cupboards.
Windows were stuck in and cut out at whim,
regardless of symmetry.
Doors were cut through,
then nailed up again when found to lead into space
twenty feet above ground.
Outbuildings were linked on by walks and grape arbors,
until the whole confusion
spraddled cheerfully over most of the hilltop.

My young son and I went through the house last summer,
with wild thoughts
of buying and restoring it.

Crepe myrtles and straggling rosevines
showed us where a garden once was.
The driveway was a memory.
Hundred-and-twenty-year-old oaks,
the saplings of 1860,
umbrella'd the sun high above us.

Wyndcliff Hall was in time abandoned
and lived to become a highway camp,
wherein dwelt many families at once.
Each family lived, cookery and all, in one room,
and cast its debris out of the handiest window spaces.

In the course of its degradation the house shrank.
Black walnut mantelpieces became kindling,
rooms collapsed, were torn off,
chopped up for firewood,
or re-erected as chicken houses.
A pig was raised, fattened and slaughtered
beneath the dooryard oaks.
Mules were tethered to peach trees.
Hounds bayed from beneath the porch.

But a house
put together with dowel pins instead of nails
and founded on beams rough hewn from virgin forest logs
does not give up easily.
Renovated, with a new owner,
it stands unshaken by the strong winds,
protected from the long-vanished highway
by the old Bishop's trees.
The walls are askew, the floors are wavy,
and the roof
remains sketchy,
but, like a true Sewanee mansion,
it never leaks twice in the same place.

The person who wrote those words in 1932
abandoned the house in his turn
after renaming it "Neverland":
as a place where great matters were once tended
and great things were yet to be done,
while the present
is a perpetual Never. . . .

The porch crumbled like dry moss under our feet.
The door dropped open to our touch.

I held my son's hand as tightly as he gripped mine
that day last summer.
Our live voices belled in those hollow rooms.
What we felt as we picked our way over broken glass
on the slanting and water-ruined floors
is hard to describe.
Something was there that resented us,
that shunned the future we embodied.
I felt it was everything that had given up hope
back in that old catastrophe,
everything not touched by the will to thrive.
Something, unspeakably different from us,
accustomed to command and now not able to,
looked testily out
at the June sun and remorseless green—
something as palpable
as the spirit of Mr. Dabney, after he died of old age at forty,
having lost his fortune in the War,
shuffling past the gate of his torn-down house at night
before electric lights, in carpet slippers.

We were glad to hear the tall weeds
slide under our chassis
as we drove out from under those shadows
into 1980.

V.

In the 1850s the founders had envisioned
broad avenues, fountains, Jeffersonian symmetries.
In the 1890s
the Gothic battlements their survivors built
served their experience,
which told them there was something to fight against,
and something to fight for.

In those dilapidated, down-at-the-heels days,
when Sewanee had one tower,
still her loveliest—
a copy of Magdalen Tower, Oxford—
one that looked capable of repelling a proper siege
among the broadleaf trees,
complete with crossbows and catapulted stones, —
a genteel versifier,
seeing the real
through the ephemera of the actual,
called the University
A towered city set within a wood,
Far from the world, upon a mountain's crest:
There storms of life break not, nor cares intrude.
There learning dwells, and peace is wisdom's guest.

But why do I let these ghosts talk
and tire you with their names and histories,
their verses,
and stories of their houses,
so that the living faces of my students
blur before my eyes?

Is it because *the present*
is a perpetual Never
and the past, detailed by memory,
pathetic because finished,
appealing to the imagination because half-imaginary,
lays its vanished, living hand on my hand
and demands to be articulated?

Or is there another reason?

My thoughts run from the past
to the future as I fear it will be—
to the bands of food-gathering nomads,
omnivorous bipeds bearing awful marks,
mouthing an eroded tongue,
who find their way through weirdly revitalized forests
to this mountaintop
looking for a stopping-place,
for water they can drink—,
when the freeways are lost to wild brambles
and New York and Atlanta are without power
forever—
when this Neo-Gothic library
has fallen into the ruins I strangely desire
(for the habit of rebellion dies hard)—
when this paper,
these many-layered words,
have ruined into grey dust that glows.

In these former buildings,
strangers out of the catastrophic future,
these traces that were roads, —
life was destroyed
and came back.
Literate people lived here,
whose sense of themselves as a nation drew breath
long after their armies disbanded;
whose pride was made homely by ruin;
who gave more than they got.

In their community the gifted and the gracious led;
but everyone had a place,
and no two people were the same;
and even fools were suffered, though never gladly, —
and laughter survived.

This was a place
where the sacraments were kept,
and people were kind—
though their fate and their times
might have made them otherwise—;
where the old names
for flowers
were remembered:
flags   heart's-ease   Confederate violets.

Two hundred yards to the west of here,
look for a limestone spring in a cave.

Note: The University of the South, called Sewanee by all who know it—after the tiny village on the Cumberland Rim where it is situated —has a small but fascinating literature. See *Purple Sewanee,* ed. Lily Baker, Charlotte Gailor, Rose Duncan Lovell, and Sarah Hodgson Torian, Association for the Preservation of Tennessee Antiquities, 1932; *Men Who Made Sewanee,* by Moultrie Guerry, updated by Arthur Ben and Elizabeth N. Chitty, The University Press, Sewanee, Tennessee, 1932, 1981; *Sewanee Cook Book,* ed. Queenie Woods Washington, Emerald-Hodgson Hospital Auxiliary, 1926, 1958; and *Sewanee Sampler,* by Arthur Ben Chitty, The University Press, Sewanee, Tennessee, 1978. Also of interest: Chapter IX, "Sewanee," from *Lanterns on the Levee,* by William Alexander Percy, Alfred A. Knopf, New York, 1941; a pamphlet, "Sewanee's Heritage: Isolation, Poverty, and Community," by the Rt. Rev. Girault M. Jones, no publisher listed; and "Sewanee: Then and Now," by Arthur Ben Chitty, *Tennessee Historical Quarterly,* Vol. XXXVIII, Winter, 1979. A little-known and out-of-print classic, *Ely: Too Black, Too White,* by Ely Green, ed. Arthur Ben and Elizabeth N. Chitty, University of Massachusetts Press, Amherst, 1970, is an autobiographical account of Sewanee in the early years of this century by one whose mixed parentage isolated him from both the white and the black communities, but whose character and spiritual dignity allowed him to prevail. The italicized passages in "Sewanee in Ruins" are taken from the works mentioned here and are used by permission. I wish to express my gratitude to Arthur Chitty and especially to Betty Chitty, who generously advised me on Sewaneeana and who were responsible for the publication of the poem as a handset, letterpress chapbook (1st edition, 1981; 2nd edition, 1983), printed by Jack Sutherland at The University Press in Sewanee.

Easter Week: Vermont

for Robert Fitzgerald

Snowbanks, exhausted, melt onto pavement.
Slick stripes on the road, buttercup yellow—
A pickup truck that color, and a sign,
Diamond-shaped, "Frost Heaves," stuck in grey snow.

In graveyards, around tombstones, snow scooped, cupped,
Around named, sun-thawed granite and marble.
The trees, from within, push back the snowdrifts.
Maybe in wild trout today the blood moves.

Maples, five feet through, drain into buckets.
A white-haired man, his black-and-red-checked back
To me, lumbers through timber with buckets full.
Steam spouts out the tops of sugar-houses.

New birch saplings by the roadside stare
With a coldness from inside the bark
That goes back a hundred million winters.
Their nerve has survived another freeze.

The bare ground, snow-covered since November,
Turns up filter-tips, newspapers bleached of print,
Blue plastic-coated wires, styrofoam cups,
A red something, a Christmas ornament.

Flinching, cowlicked, stunned by the six-months' winter,
The grass flushes tawny, deep amethyst,
And keeps its eyes shut to the light.
An alder's leafless crown colors redly.

The landscape, in that old and simple way
Of saying just what happens, "awakens."
It renews itself like the unfolding
Fine linen of stored words heard once a year:

Mary Magdalene and the other Mary
At daybreak on the first day of the week
Came unto that fresh-cut word the sepulchre.
The stone, the vowels sing, was rolled away.

Two men stand by them in shining garments.
He is not here, they say. *He is risen.*
Why seek ye the living among the dead?
Tough-stemmed crocuses stir underfoot.

Envoi

Go little book, *par avion.*
Wing, verses, toward your targets:
Where faces cool and harden behind bars,
Where an idea straps on a pistol,

Where the people eat their right to vote,
Where machine guns and TV cameras
Look from the tops of glass buildings.
Go, little peregrine.

Fly as I taught you
With bombs tucked under your wings,
In a V of attack, low to the ground,
Underneath the enemy's lazy radar. . . .

It's too much though—isn't it, little friend?
You glide over cool marble floors
Out into the womanly moonlight.
A rosevine encircles you, you bleed on the thorns.

Your throat opens to a harmony of seasons.
You sing of the nest, of unruffled June mornings,
Of leaving the nest, of building it again;
Of its perfect circle.

You would have me kill, you whose life is a breath?
I pity you, yes I pity you, you warble,
And take off into the distance
As if you thought you would live forever.

I stand in the predawn field, boots drenched,
The big glove covering my wrist and hand,
And watch you soar, a speck now,
Into the rainy future.

About the Author

Born during World War II in Memphis, Richard Tillinghast is the author of *Sleep Watch* (1969) and *The Knife and Other Poems* (1980), both published by Wesleyan. He has taught at Harvard, Sewanee, Berkeley, and San Quentin Prison. He writes regularly on poetry for *The Nation, The New York Times Book Review,* and *The Washington Post,* and is associate professor of English at the University of Michigan. He lives in Ann Arbor.

About the Book

Our Flag Was Still There has been composed in Linotron 202 Bembo by Carolinatype. It was printed on 60 lb. Warren's Olde Style. It was printed and bound at Kingsport Press. The jackets and covers were printed by New England Book Components. It was designed and produced by Joyce Kachergis Book Design and Production.